My World

Size

Ruth Merttens

Raintree

www.raintreepublishers.co.uk
Visit our website to find out more information about **Raintree** books.

To order:
☎ Phone 44 (0) 1865 888112
📄 Send a fax to 44 (0) 1865 314091
💻 Visit the Heinemann Bookshop at **www.raintreepublishers.co.uk** to browse our catalogue and order online.

First published in Great Britain by Raintree, Halley Court, Jordan Hill, Oxford OX2 8EJ, part of Harcourt Education.
Raintree is a registered trademark of Harcourt Education Ltd.

Editorial: Charlotte Guillain and Diyan Leake
Design: Michelle Lisseter
Picture Research: Maria Joannou
Production: Lorraine Hicks

Originated by Dot Gradations
Printed and bound in China by South China Printing Company

ISBN 1 844 21269 6
07 06 05 04 03
10 9 8 7 6 5 4 3 2 1

British Library Cataloguing in Publication Data
Merttens, Ruth
Size
516.1′5
A full catalogue record for this book is available from the British Library.

Acknowledgements
The publishers would like to thank the following for permission to reproduce photographs: NHPA/Alan Barnes pp. **20**, **21a**; NHPA/Ant Photo Library pp. **12**, **13a**; RSPCA Photolibrary pp. **10**, **11a**; Tudor Photography pp. **4**, **5**, **6**, **7**, **8**, **9**, **11b**, **13b**, **14**, **15**, **16**, **17**, **18**, **19**, **21b**, **22**, **23**, **24**.

Cover photograph, reproduced with permission of Pete Morris.

Every effort has been made to contact copyright holders of any material reproduced in this book. Any omissions will be rectified in subsequent printings if notice is given to the publishers.

Contents

Some words are shown in bold, **like this.** You can find them in the glossary on page 24.

How big are you?

Everyone says how big you are getting.

Do you know how tall you are?

You can use a **chart** to find out how tall you are.

Are you bigger than this dog?

This is a Great Dane.

A Great Dane is a very big dog.

Are you bigger than this horse?

This is a cart horse.

A cart horse is a very big, strong horse.

Are you bigger than an elephant?

This is an African elephant.

Elephants are the biggest land animals in the world.

Are you bigger than a whale?

This is a humpback whale.

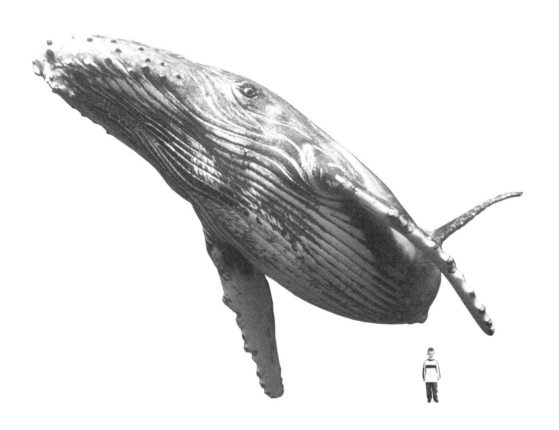

Whales are the biggest animals in the world.

Are you bigger than this horse?

This is a Shetland pony.

A Shetland pony is the smallest horse there is.

Are you bigger than this dog?

This is a Yorkshire terrier.

A Yorkshire terrier is quite a small dog.

Are you bigger than a cat?

This is a black and white cat.

Most pet cats are quite small.

Are you bigger than a butterfly?

This is a silver-studded blue butterfly.

Butterflies are quite small.

So, what size are you?

This dog is really big.

Are you bigger than this dog?

This dog is quite small.

Are you bigger than this dog?

Glossary

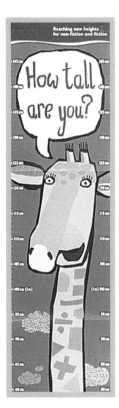

chart
record showing special information like how tall you are

Index